AF601411

NURSES ARE PATIENT PEOPLE

By Eloise Schwarz

AuthorHouse™
1663 Liberty Drive
Bloomington, IN 47403
www.authorhouse.com
Phone: 1 (800) 839-8640

Published by AuthorHouse 07/06/2017

ISBN: 978-1-4208-6908-8 (sc)
ISBN: 978-1-4678-5279-1 (e)

Print information available on the last page.

authorHOUSE®

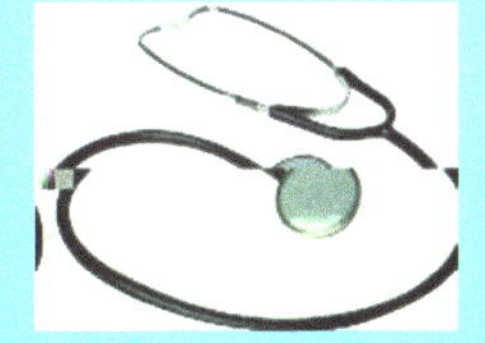

NURSES ARE PATIENT PEOPLE

What is a *Nurse*?

Can you draw a picture of a *nurse*? If you could, what would your *nurse* look like?

Perhaps, a male *nurse* or a lady *nurse* with a chart in her hand and a stethoscope (STETH-uh-skope*)* around her neck. Would your *nurse* be dressed in a white uniform (U-ni-form) with white tennis shoes?

This type of drawing would show what some *nurses* may look like. But there are many different kinds of *nurses*. Some wear scrub-type uniforms. Some wear colorful pant uniforms. Some even wear business suits for their job. *Nurses* are special people who care about many different human beings, no matter what type of uniform they wear.

What *Nurses* Do

Nurses are one type of a special group of professional (Pro-FESH-i-nals) health care workers. Doctors, dentists and therapists (THER-a-pests) are professionals also. They all need a special education to do their jobs.

Nurses are smart people with many talents. They take care of sick people. They also know how to help healthy people stay well.

Nurses are responsible for teaching people about eating properly, exercising and taking their medicine correctly. *Nurses* listen, give help and comfort. *Nurses* even give gentle hugs to show that they care and understand.

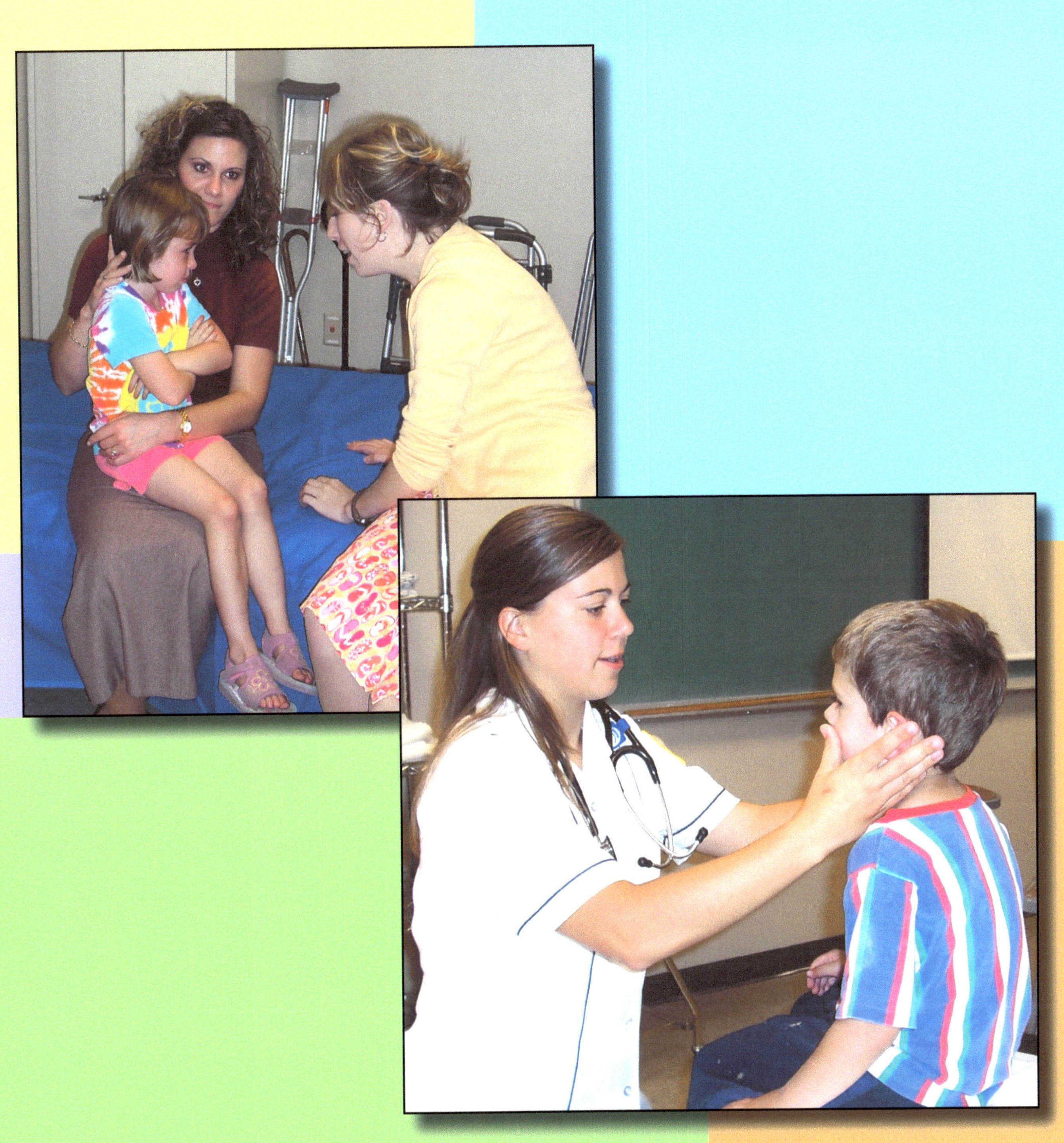

Different Kinds of *Nurses*

Nurses can choose to work in any type of special area of nursing. Some *nurses* love to work with children and are called Pediatric (PE-de-at-ric) *Nurses*. Other *nurses* work with the old people. They are called Geriatric (Ger-ri-A-tric) *nurses*. Your school *nurse* is a Public Health *Nurse*.

Nurses work many different hours. Hospitals and nursing homes never close. They need *nurses* to work during the day time and the night time. Clinics and schools are open during the day time. *Nurses* work hard but can still find time to have fun.

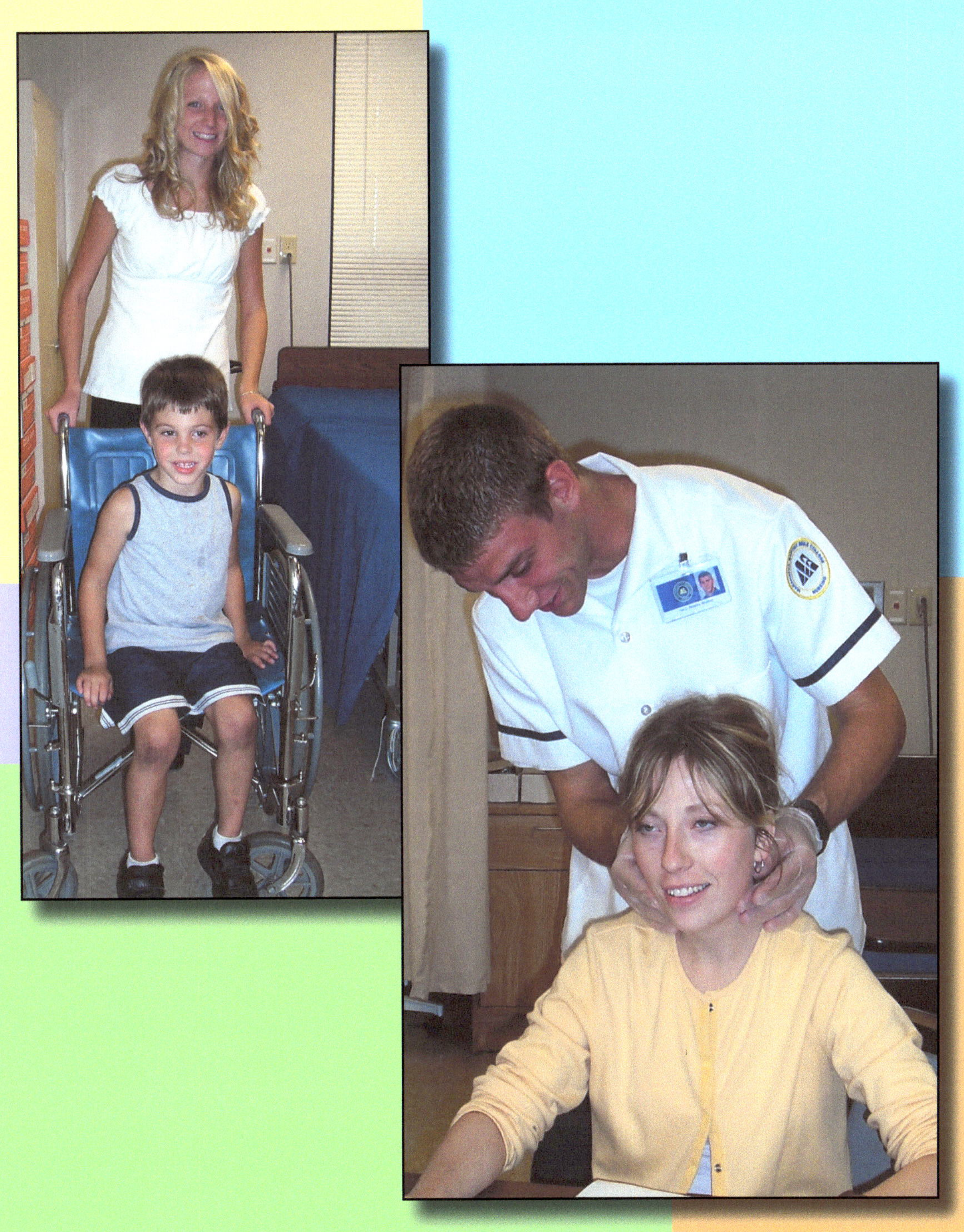

Where Do *Nurses* Work

Nurses work in many different places. They can take care of babies, children, older people and even you. Hospitals (HOS-pi-tals*)* have the most *nurses*. They can work in the Intensive Care Unit (ICU) (in-TEN-siv-care*)* or the Emergency Room (ER) (e-MER-gen-cy-room*)* where the really sick people are taken care of. If you need an operation *(*OP-er-a-shun*)*, *nurses* are also there to help the doctors take care of you and to keep you safe.

There are other places that *nurses* work. Your doctor's office has *nurses*. They take your temperature and weigh you before you see your doctor. *Nurses* also work in nursing homes, jails, schools, and even insurance companies.

Have you met your school *nurse*?

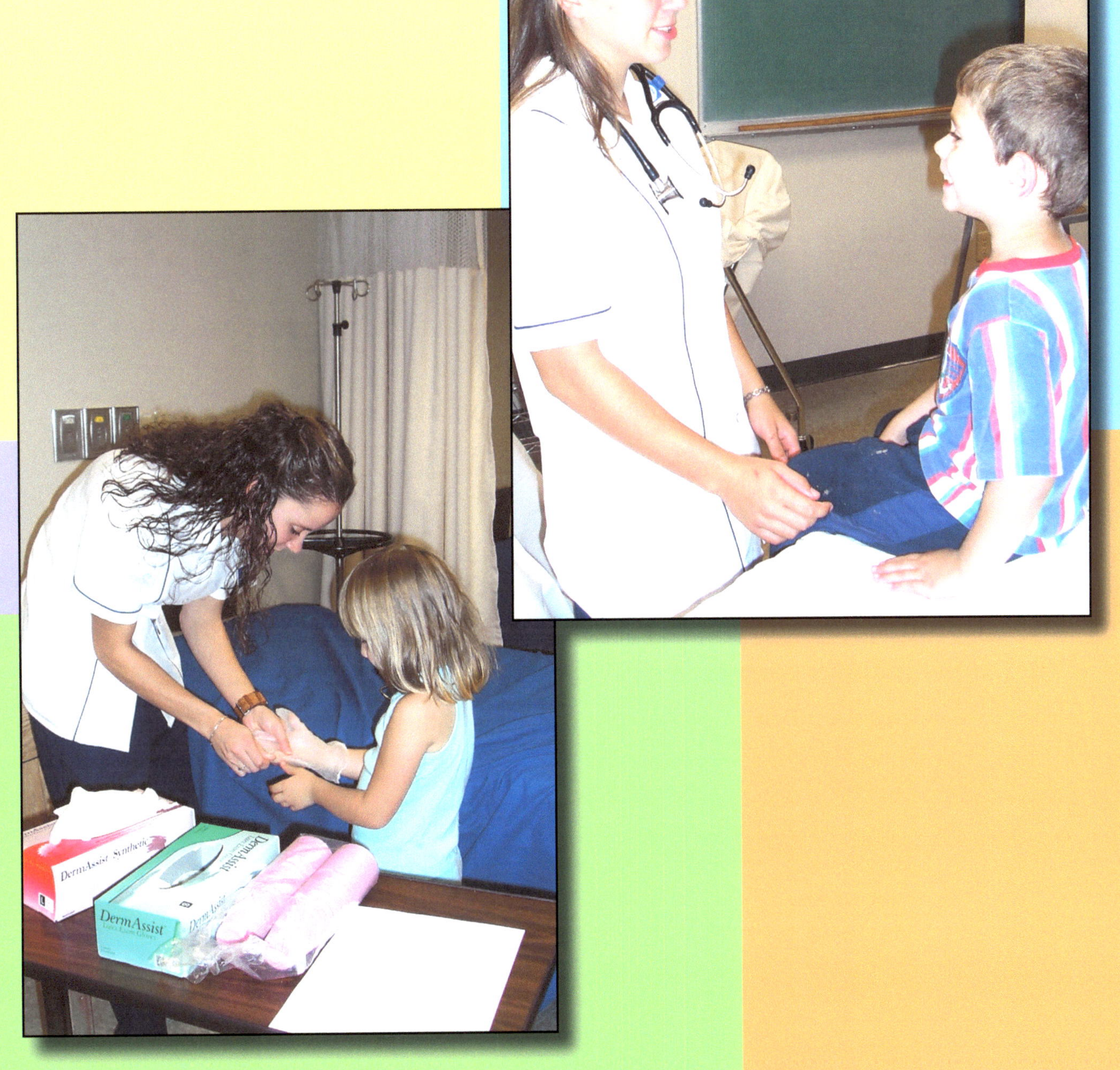
DermAssist Synthetic
DermAssist

Becoming a *Nurse*

High school graduates (GRAD-u-ates) can become *nurses* when they finish 2 to 5 years of college. *Nurses* need to take a national board exam (test) after they are done with school. When they pass, they can work as a *Registered Nurse* (RE-gi-ster-ed nur se).

Nurses study science, math and health. *Nurses* use these tools for taking your vital signs (VYE-tuhl-sinz). They use a thermometer (thur-MOM-uh-tur), stethoscope (STETH-uh-skope), and a blood pressure cuff. Vital signs include your pulse, breathing, blood pressure and temperature. *Nurses* even use computers, cell phones and pagers to do their jobs.

Fast Facts:

Career Title: Registered Nurse

Education: 2 to 5 years college

Certificate: State License/Exam

U.S. Salary: $35,000 - $90,000 [depending on location, education and experience]

U.S. Job Outlook: **EXCELLENT**

Being a nurse may be hard work but they know it is important to help other people. Nurses are *patient* people with a heart for serving others.

Do YOU want to be a nurse?

Health Advice

EXERCISE your body naturally - run, stretch, hop, walk and run

EXERCISE your mind - read, think, dream and talk

GET a good night's sleep - your body slows down and heals itself

BREATHE through your nose - it cleans, warms and conditions the air before it reaches your lungs

EAT delicious and nutritious foods -fruits, vegetables, milk, breads, cereals, meat and eggs

CHEW your food well - makes it easy for your stomach to work better

KEEP your teeth clean - brush after each meal and floss every day

DRINK plenty of WATER

WASH your hands often - keep the GERMS away

Words to Know

COLLEGE: a school that is higher than high school

CLINIC: a doctor's office where people are seen and taken care of when sick or hurt

EXAM: a test

HEALTH: freedom from illness

HOSPITAL: a place where doctors and nurses take care of people who are sick or hurt

MATHEMATICS (math): the study of numbers, measurements and shapes

PROFESSIONAL: a person who has a job that requires special education

REGISTERED NURSE: a trained nurse who has passed a State examination

STETHOSCOPE: an instrument used by doctors and nurses to listen to heartbeats and other sounds in the body

THERAPIST: a trained person who helps people to heal

UNIFORM: special or official clothes that a person of a special group wears

Internet Sites

FUN WITH FOOD:
http://www.funwithfood.com/kidsclub.html

KIDS HEALTH:
http://kidshealth.org/kid/index.html

YUCKY GROSS & COOL BODY:
http://www.yucky.com/body

SCIENCE & TECHNOLOGY - Children:
http://www.ala.org/parentspage/greatsites/science.html

KEEP KIDS HEALTHY:
http://www.keepkidshealthy.com

WALKING: http://www.walking.org

BRAIN FITNESS:
http://faculty.washington.edu/chudler/brainfit.html

This book is dedicated to all future *nurses.*

NURSES

Are

PATIENT

PEOPLE

Have you
hugged your
nurse today?

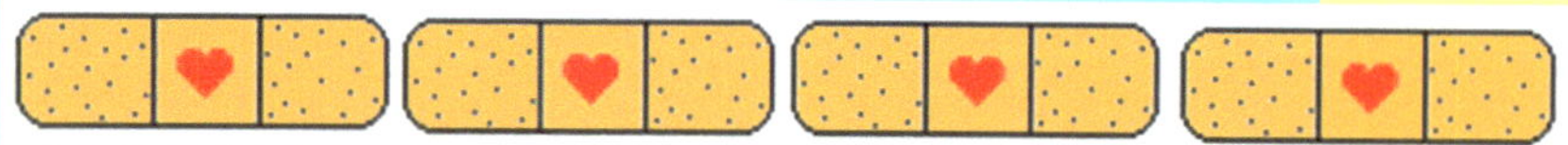

NURSES
Are Patient People

A Children's Book about Nursing

By

NURSE
Eloise Schwarz

Project for MBA 590 - Concordia University Wisconsin

March 16, 2003

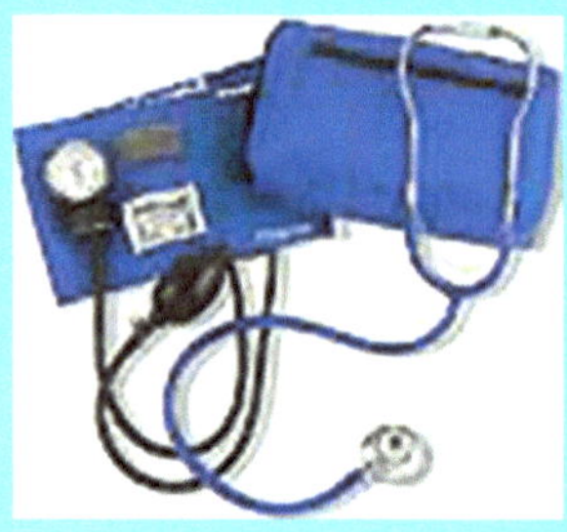

About the Author

I am a Registered Nurse with 30+ years in nursing - employed in all areas of service from pediatrics to geriatrics. Hospital, clinic, workers compensation, home care, private duty, as well as insurance settings have all contributed a greater understanding and knowledge base as well as a deeper appreciation for the many hats a nurse wears in her lifetime.

Certified in Case Management as well as Parish Nursing, I have trumpeted the role of servicing all those in need. Consultant and teacher add yet another focus and target for peers and community contacts.

In my master's studies, the theme of our nationally recognized and long-suffering nursing shortage became my focused banner. Taking a stand, voicing my opinion and showing a passion for the profession became my thesis. As a guest author, a specialty article on the nursing shortage was published on the Medscape Nursing website.

This child's book is yet another direction in bringing to mind that nursing is also a profession to be considered, even at the elementary level. In my research prior to writing this book for my capstone class, I was disappointed to learn that few books had been written about nursing for the young reader. Surrounded by many eye-catching professions, such as firemen, police and doctors, focused but simple information on nursing was lacking or targeted for the older student.

This small user-friendly hands-on book appeals to children in pictures, new health-oriented words with phonics for easy pronunciation and websites that actually work. The intention is to draw the young reader, 9 to 11 years of age, to consider, reflect, and explore the profession of nursing.

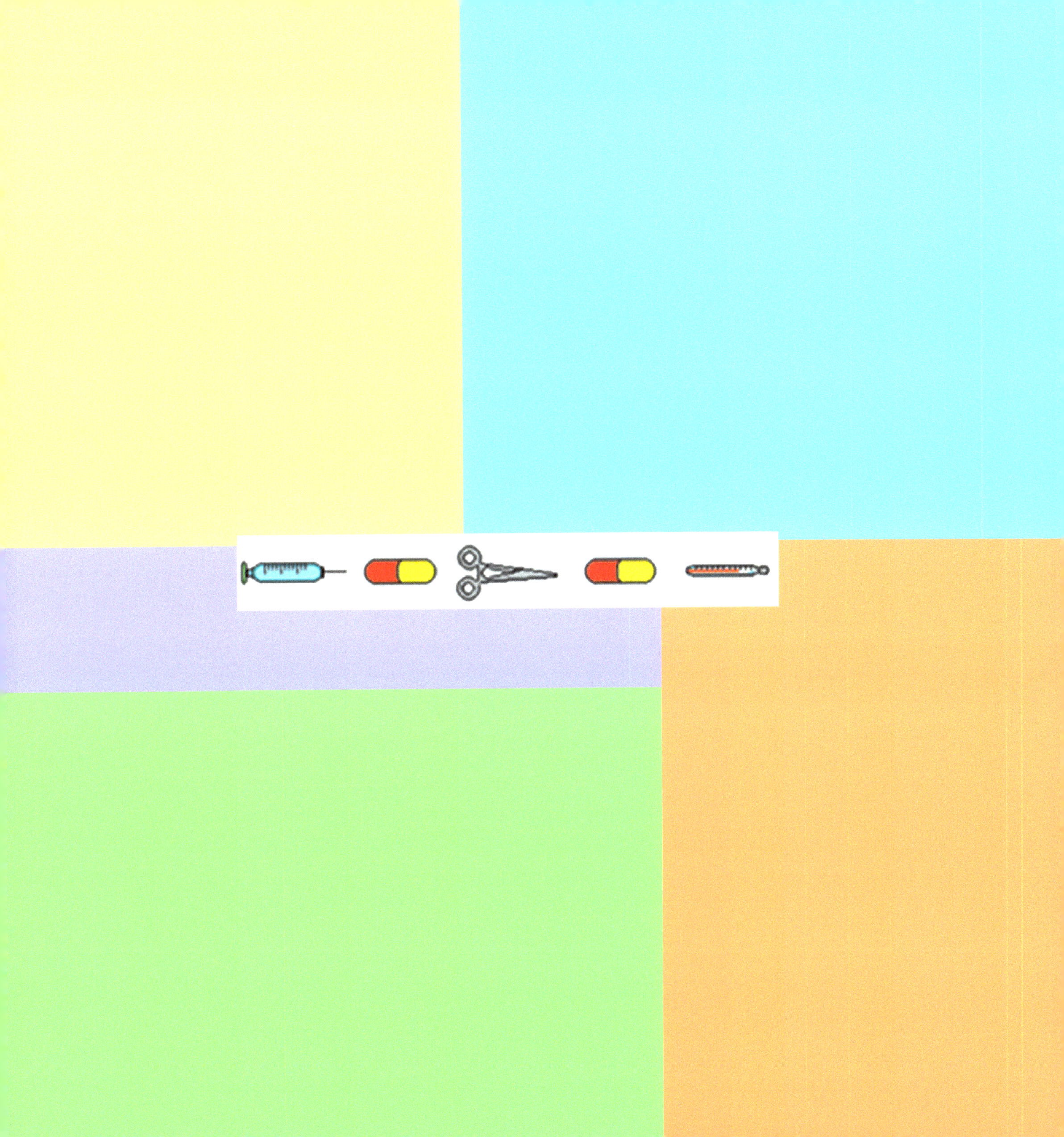

www.ingramcontent.com/pod-product-compliance
Ingram Content Group UK Ltd.
Pitfield, Milton Keynes, MK11 3LW, UK
UKHW060115300726
14090UKWH00002B/202

* 9 7 8 1 4 2 0 8 6 9 0 8 8 *